Prese

Written by Lisa Trumbauer

CELEBRATION PRESS
Pearson Learning Group

Our world today is very different than it was a hundred years ago. Today we have computers and televisions. Airplanes soar across the sky. Buildings tower in big cities. Cars zoom down paved roads.

Machines were invented to make life easier. Today we have washing machines, dishwashers, refrigerators, and microwave ovens. Our world changes with each new invention. Can you imagine what life was like before these inventions?

Today we flip a switch, and we have light. This light is made with electricity. It took many years for people to learn how to use electricity. In the past, people used candles for light.

Light of the Present

Light of the Past

4

Today we turn a knob on an oven and quickly cook our food. Or we push buttons on a microwave oven for an even quicker meal. In the past, people cooked their food in large fireplaces and brick ovens.

Cooking in the Present

Cooking in the Past

Keeping Food Cool in the Present

Today we have refrigerators that keep foods fresh and cold. The food can last longer. It doesn't spoil as quickly.

In the past, people didn't have refrigerators. Instead, food was often stored in cool, underground cellars.

Keeping Food Cool in the Past

Today we have machines to wash and dry our clothes. We put the clothes inside, push a few buttons, and the machines do most of the work.

In the past, people washed their clothes by hand. They placed a washboard in a big round tub filled with water. They scrubbed the clothes on the board to get them clean. Then they hung them out to dry.

Doing the Wash in the Present

Doing the Wash in the Past

7

Communicating in the Present

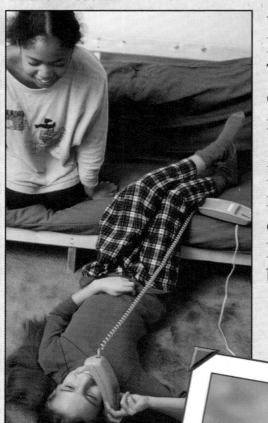

Today we have telephones so we can talk to people who live far away. Telephones help us communicate with friends and family.

In the past there were no telephones. People communicated over long distances mostly by writing letters.

Communicating in the Past

8

Today people still write letters, and mail carriers still deliver the mail. But today we can also send letters over the telephone lines. This is what happens when we send E-mail. The computer is hooked up to a phone line. The letter travels over the telephone line from one person's computer to another person's computer.

Today we get from place to place by riding in cars. Cars allow us to travel more quickly. Cars allow us to travel with our friends and family.

Cars have changed over the years. Here is a car from about 40 years ago.

Car From 1960s

Here is a car from about 70 years ago.

Car From 1930s

Here is one of the earliest cars. It was called the Model-T. It came out in 1908.

Model-T From 1908

11

Traveling by Covered Wagon

Traveling by Horse and Carriage

What did people do before cars? They used horses to help them get from place to place. Horses pulled the covered wagons that moved the pioneers across the country. Horses pulled carriages through towns and cities.

Horses also pulled "trains." They pulled wagons that rolled on rails. Then the steam engine was invented. New trains were then powered by steam. These new trains did not need any horses. Today trains are powered by electricity.

Train of the Past

Train of the Present

In the past, people didn't travel by plane. Planes hadn't been invented yet. But people liked to experiment with ways to fly.

14

Today we see planes soar across the sky. Without those early experiments in flight, we might not have the planes of today.

Friends of the Present

Friends of the Past

With each new invention, our world changes. The world of the present is different from the world of the past. Some things, however, do stay the same.